Simcha to Shiva

---

poems in my time

Sterling Clarren

Copyright © 2017 by Sterling Clarren

All rights reserved. No part of this publication may be reproduced, distributed or transmitted in any form without the prior written permission of the publisher, except in the case of brief quotations embodied in critical reviews.

1st edition.

ISBN 9780692874851
LCCN 2017905451

Published by Paisley Cellars Press
Printed by Village Books in Bellingham, WA, USA

This book is dedicated to my family and the places we live and roam.

*Remembering times of celebration,
contemplation, dreams and death*

Poems from my early 21st century life

My 20th century life went by in what would have seemed from a distance as a pretty straight line of academic achievement leading to a successful career, living in a solid marriage and raising two wonderful kids in a secure community of friends. There was a lot of hard work, with planning and struggle on all fronts, of course, but things went along more or less as expected. Then came the new millennium and there was a job opportunity in Canada and a move, other travel to far off places, challenging health problems for my wife and for me, and watching children grow up, develop their own careers, find mates and have children. People got sick, people died. Adventures abounded. Life in the new millennium became so much richer and so much more out of control.

I have had a habit of dating my poems to the time I finished their first full drafts. I have put them together by the months of their origin, forming one solar orbit in my personal life cycle journey. They are all stuffed in this book like the events they recall are all stuffed in my head. So start anywhere and finish when you wish. Perhaps you can pretend that you and I are walking together and I am telling you a random tale or two stimulated by a smell or sound, the season of the year or perhaps a connection in our real or imagined relationship. May you find one or two that delight you, confuse you or just make you wonder.

L'chaim,

Sterling Clarren

Table of Contents

September

Erev Rosh Hashanah and Jonathan 12
A Stroll Along the Nooksack 13
Bampy Awaiting 14
Jewish Eternity 15
Toast to the Marriage of Rebecca and Gregory 16
Yahrzeit for David 18

October

Nunavut Sojourn 22
Yom Kippur Reverie 23
Family Fun 24
Oh God, Oh No 25

November

Prenuptial Toast for Katharine and Jonathan 28
Happy 100th Birthday Granny Pearl 29
Cuban Sunrise 32
Aging 33
Oh, Lord, it is I 34

December

Friday Night 36
Transplant at 4911 37

January

The Hunters of Playa Escondido 40
May I be Excused 41
New Years Morning 42
Cabin Pressure 43
To an Old Friend 44

February

Upon Hearing of the Terminal Illness of our Mother 46
Recital 47
Walking the Labyrinth at Rancho La Puerta 48
Shabbat in Cancer Land 49

March

Retiring from the Canada FASD Research Network 52
Mantra for Trainer Rachel 53
Kahuwai Downpour 54
Make a Wish 55
Solace 56
The Hex 57
The Wall 58
Cheerios, Billy Collins and Being 70 59

April

The Miracle of You 62
Recital Responsa 63
Maui Day Break with Becca 64
Absalom, oh, Absalom 65

May

Retired 68
Snit Fit 69
Doctor, Tell Me 70
Why I Hike 71
Tryst 72
To Sandy 73
Outing 74
Out to Lunch 75

June

Rebecca, Daughter of the Summer Solstice 78
Wedding Dance 79
Vincent Avenue North, 1951 80
Summer Shower 81
The Carnival Ride 82
Toast at a Family Wedding 84

July

Canada Geese 86
Bad Day for Butterflies 87
From Diablo Lake 88
Time for Healing 90
Life is a Beach 91
Biking the Bay 92
Time Squared 93

August

Piggies 96
Poets on the High Divide 97
The Decider 98
August Question 99
Red and Steamy 100
Dockside 101
High Mountain Huckleberries 102
Syncope at the County Concert 103
Cloudburst 104
Haiku in the Forest 105
Ross Lake Sunrise 106
Penultimate Poem 107
Cycles End 108

Poems in alphabetical order 110
Poems in chronological order 112
Glossary of Hebrew and Yiddish words used 114

September

Erev Rosh Hashanah and Jonathan

He was dying or
That is what he thought.
Asthma, again,
And now it seemed his
Throat would close.

He studied the ceiling as
The ER team
Used the drugs that
Brought him back.

Tomorrow
His parents would go alone
For tashlikh while he
Lay coughing.

What could they confess?
As the ducks, greedy,
Ate the bread,
Knowing not their assignments.

Walking home
They would find blackberries
Ripe on the hill,
Sweet as the late, fair weather.

He would eat from their pail.
Hungry in recovery.
Old asthma, like the shofar,
Blaring in the New Year.

A Stroll Along the Nooksack

In the forest by the creek
I fall behind to see

The bounce of her hair
That sways with every step.

As sun drips from redding leaves
And drops on mossy stones,

She turns and smiles,
Are you Okay? Oh yes, I am.

Bampy Awaiting

You came to me in the dream.
I saw your face, your mother's nose,
Your father's lips and great big feet.
The serenity in your cuddled frame.

It must be wonderful to float and float,
To hear your mother's song,
To feel your father's gentle pats,
To be warm and safe as you will never be again.

But come out little one, come out and play.
I know it is cold and scratchy,
That there will be pangs of hunger,
Spasms of frustrated fury.

You know you are not sure,
But come out and play.
Meet this wild world
That is ready to embrace you.

Jewish Eternity
thoughts before the days of awe

"And at the end of days
You will be united with
Family members long dead"

In a dream, they came to me.
To let me know the time was soon
And I must prepare.

Forever
With an uncle who hates,
A father who bullies,
A grandmother, self-absorbed?

Endless
Dinner arguments
Matched to long silences
Boring little games?

Continuous
Competition for space and time
And who really cares?
Or so it always feels.

Who among us could believe
In death they would be different?
Why should we think so?

Ah, I see, it isn't heaven.

Toast to the Marriage of Rebecca and Gregory

Your children grow up
And they do what they do
And you try to be careful
And try to be true
To the path that you hope
They will follow

Your children grow up
And they find their own friends
They find lovers and clingers
Women and men
Who help them and hurt them
As you follow

Your children grow up
And they find their own voice
They take issue with you
They define their own choice
They pick this and grab that leaving
You wondering

Then your children grow up
And propose to a mate
That fills you with awe
At the turn in their fate
And you look at the two
And you know it

Some how in this world
Souls find a true match
This Becca and Greg
Put the key in that latch
And opened the door
To their heaven

Your children grow up
And the day is then found
When you say to yourself
Well the world's not so round
But these two are ready
To help it

So you raise your tall glass
With pride in these two
You wish them God's speed
In the things they will do
And the love that they share in
Their world for tomorrow

My Becca, My Greg
With all the love in my heart
I love each of you
But the sum of the parts
Is far greater than anything
That I imagined

Your families and friends
Are here joining with you
In this celebration
Of that which is new
And our heartfelt embraces
You've earned them, you two

Yahrzeit for David

My father was no safe haven.
His voice could be breaking thunder,
His face a cloud of rage,
His body taut with violent fury.

He was as hard on us
As a battering surf.
He was as distant from us
As a coastal isle.

As he blew into the house
We could not know if today's hurricane
Would strike or veer away.
How much high wind damage tonight?

So when he died, I put his
Watch upon my wrist,
His jacket on my shoulders,
And his knife into my pocket.

Yet his gear could not protect me
From the storm that still could rage.
Had my blustery father made travel
To his shore impossible forever?

But I remembered lulls when I was young
And he would sit on the yellow sofa,
In the early evening with the big, big
Book of children's verse.

He would sit
And we could sit, not too far away,
Or over look his shoulder,
Or lie upon the floor.

There were poems of Robinson
And Poe, Frost and de la Mare
And always the pleasure
Of our best loved, Ogden Nash.

And somewhere in the red weather
Of those distant evenings,
We could all just be together
And feel the gentle breeze.

Memories lay like the torn up path
Of a spent tornado.
We can pick through the ruins and
Take those remains we need to keep.

October

Nunavut Sojourn

When you find Kugluktuk,
The wind will find you
And will scream your name
And grab your shoulders.

It will hammer the sleet
To your eyebrows
And stiffen your fingers
In the leather of your gloves.

Perhaps you will howl like the dogs
In the night who sing the song
Of the wind. As if this harmony
Could mean coexistence.

Hide as you will behind a blind.
Wrap yourself in skins and blankets.
Even igloos tumble down in days.
Easier to live on the moon.

Kick your boot tip at the Arctic ice.
Find a stone from near the shore.
Say farewell and fly from here.
The wind will speed you on away.

Yom Kippur Reverie

A
Tree was
Planted near my grave. In
Spring I saw the three came marching.
Jude was leading them to prune the limbs
And tend the ground. They came running back again in Fall.
Louie leaping hard to climb and grab first ripeness. Eyes so bright and
Laughing as the sweet juice dribbled down his chin. But
         Little   Livi
brought
the
basket
and
bid
them
collect
the
fruit,
And then with
Shy, sure smile said, and let's go bake a pie!

Family Fun

My sister phoned to tell me
What they told her not to tell.
She called me just to tell me
Though it might send her to hell.

My brother's only daughter
Has been suing for divorce.
The kids are newly married
And they hardly stayed the course.

Mother thinks its awful bad,
But isn't 'sposed to show it.
Older sister thinks its fair,
But isn't 'spose to know it.

Frankly I don't really care
Though that view just won't fly.
So I will show a long, sad face
But pretend I don't know why.

It gets harder at the holidays
To recall what "I don't know."
To smile and seem oblivious,
But that's the row we hoe.

Oh God, Oh No

                    she cries out from our restless slumber
                    yowling like the dogs beyond the fence
                    Oh God, Oh No! and I try not to move
                    but listen to her breathing as the signal
                    to reach for her or to feign my sleeping
                    as first bird song portends the morning
                    I open my eye to meet her opened eyes

November

Prenuptial toast for Katharine and Jonathan

Everyone in this room loves you so.
We all await two turning three.
We're so happy and glad for you both.
We wish joy for your new family.

Tomorrow you both say your vows.
The setting will surely be grand.
I hear that you wrote them yourselves.
I know it will go off as you planned.

Parental concerns can seem lame,
Though our intentions are only for right.
We want you to evolve and to grow
And your life, as a pair, to be bright.

So now is the time for my prayer:
May you always have each other's back.
May you learn to ever fight fair.
May your love for each other n'er slack.

I've written this poem as a verse,
So it might have a light-hearted ring.
But our hopes for you both are as wide as the sky,
May angels smile upon you and sing!

Happy 100th Birthday, Granny Pearl

Here she sits
Turning blind eyes
Trying to meet
Our board grins.
What do we see
On her special day?
After all these years
Where to begin?
Do we see the young wife
Sending her young man
Off to bend pipe and melt lead
Saving the dollar
And bearing the girls
And cleaning the house
And cooking the food
And saving the dollar
And sending her man
Off day after day
And supporting the schul
And watching the girls
And saving the dollar
And dreaming with him?
Do we see the young grandma
Holding the babes
And guiding young lives
And telling them tales
And cooking the food
That smells of the past
And holding them tight
And telling them how
To grow straight and tall
And planning their days
And cooking for simchas
That happened a lot and
Laughing and praying
And dreams coming true?
And parties and parties
All made with great joy

And cousins and cousins
Hangin' around
Watching the ball games
And playing with cards
And schmoozing and schmoozing
Long after it's dark
And moving on up
To new homes in the burbs
With fancy bath fixtures
And shiny new cars
And diamonds and minks
And freezers with food
And ovens for cooking
And baking and cooking
And sewing small things
For wee tots to enjoy
And sending her man
Off day after day
And calling the girls
And checking on all
And putting the dime
In the box for the call
To the Lord and
Thanking Him first
For all that He'd done
But badgering too
Lest He forget the next thing
That she needed
For helping her young
With a dream
And moving to Florida
And life by the shore
And getting a tan that
You can't get no more
And making new friends
In the warm sunny south
And living in peace for a while
Do we see the grandma who lost
Child and spouse
And all of the others
Who have left one by one

But kept herself going
Day after day for
One hundred years
By marking her blessings
And guarding her flock
And trying by her lights
To help those that she loved
Move towards the next simcha
Which still happens a lot
No matter the sorrowing tears
Put a coin in the pushke
And talk to your God
And tell Him how grateful you are
For the lives that we've had
And the family we've known
For the highs and lows
And the days after days
That we all go to work
And have a good meal
And hug a loved one
And keep dreaming
Everyone in this room
Has been changed by
This soul who now sits
Here and listens to us
The gifts of her life
Have spanned all of our days
We cannot thank her enough.

Cuban Sunrise

In the tropical heat
Frozen land in time, now melting.
People waking from induced slumber.

Still in bed with tousled head.
Yawning, scratching
Thinking of coffee, opening an eye.

Inheritors of grandma's house.
Living now the olden days through
Rust, fade, dust, and crumble.

What to mend, to toss,
To choose, to help?
Oh, where to start?

Rolling back over for 10 more minutes.
The alarm is blaring.
They must arise, they will begin.

Aging

One course single hair
Plucked away from lobe of ear
Now becoming white

Oh, Lord, it is I

Old men
Sip slowly
Sitting with pillows
Near windows

Rummy eyed
Watching cats
While dozing off
Or looking at the clouds

Old men
Stew about
The life that was
Or the one that wasn't

Sometimes trying
The old moves
Carefully
Perhaps painfully

Old men
Sit together on benches
Waiting for women
With more of a lifeline

Old men
Stay on the deck
Holding the main sheet
While the ship still drifts away

December

Friday night

Gathered at the table
Wife, children, partners,
A baby passed arm to arm.
Chatter, giggles,
Platters of food,
A bit of wine dropped
On the cloth.

I look at her
Farthest away and
Nearest to me
Catch her eye
And she smiles
The candles
Dance in her eyes

Transplant at 4811
tribute to Gramps

>We eviscerated her, pulling
>Guts from cavity, she
>Shimmered pearly, deathly white
>Lacking her blackened entrails.
>
>The new organ, blood red,
>Without fetid smell
>Or strains of age
>Cut now to proper shape.
>
>Deftly placed, the
>Flapper valve was flushed:
>Swoosh, Plop, Gurgle, Silence
>Mechanism of relief, restored.

January

The Hunters of Playa Escondido

False dawn turns first light
And the pelican squadron
In tight fighter formation
Floats south along the shoreline,
Inches above water,
Just behind the crested waves.

Mid morn brings the beauty
From Chicago who has
The deep tan made in a
Shop in the cold and is now
Languidly oiling her
Nearly naked body.

The pelicans will later fly north
Idly, randomly,
Wings in the fumaroles.
Some have gorging pouches.
Some land on boulders
To stare, intense, at the surf.

As the sylph joins the man
She brought down to the shore
Holding, jumping, pushing
Him gaily in the surf. Diving over him,
Letting her body touch his, casually,
Holding his gaze on her lipsticked mouth.

May I Be Excused

May I be excused? I've had enough.
We'd say at dinner
Before our father would give permission
For us to leave the table.
I don't recall him ever saying no.

Only now, it occurs to me
That I could have used that line
So often in meetings,
Business, family affairs.
May I be excused? I've had enough.

Then too with the cancer,
Doctors, treatments,
Pain and exhaustion
I could have said,
May I be excused? I've had enough.

What would have happened if I had?

New Years Morning

"Lets make love."
"I need some coffee."
"Is that how it is now,
Coffee before
And a cigarette after?"
"You know I don't smoke."

I know that.

As Beethoven's ninth
Plays on the radio,
And the sun comes peeking
Through the still drawn shade.
I roll over, grab the paper
And start the puzzles.

Cabin Pressure

The Fire Marshall condemned the flue
Aborting latent pyroclastics

A new gas insert should be the thing,
But wife and kids said "wood"

I was outvoted though I pay the bills
Well that's democracy for you

It took all summer to find the stove
Get it in and restore the mantle

Then space to organize a shed
Get the gear and store the bottles

There is a lot of wood 'round here
But hours it takes to find and stack it

Now I build the fire in the morn
After cleaning glass and sweeping ashes

I've learned how to stoke the logs
And keep it glowing all day long

Then I sit and stare as orange waves
Pulse from reddened clefts

The stove works fine, but seems to burn
More of my time than fuel

But time is what the mountains teach
And keeping warm

To an Old Friend

Here's to our friend, Old Ken Weinberg.
Glad he's still alive
So I can now get off the chair
To give the guy some jive.
Can you remember when we met?
No? Neither, I guess, can I.
It was so very long ago
And why should we even try?

The point is, we are to celebrate
This fine event with you,
Because it is together that we all
Have made it through.
We have grown into each other's lives
And hearts, if not each other brains.
Friends we are, and friends will be,
'Til little left remains.

But such talk is for another day.
Tonight we will be merry,
And celebrate this milestone
In your trek to Charon's ferry.
Damn, there I go again
Ruminatin' on your age.
It is just so hard avoiding
This changing, aging stage.

So I think that I'll shut up
By raising high my glass,
And hope that you can lift yours too
With a hint of old school dash.
And I will wish with others
Words that are so ever true,
Happy Birthday, Old Ken Weinberg,
Happy Birthday to you.

February

Upon Hearing of the Terminal Illness of Our Mother

Lila, the Night with the sunny smile,

The one who always thought "yes".
The one who said that you could.
The one who really asked "why?"
The one who knew you were good.

The one who never looked back
And ever was planning ahead.
The one who worried for you,
Having listened to what you just said.

The one who held us all close
And hugged us dear and so tight.
Squeeze, Squash, Apple Sauce.
Good Night, Dear Lila, Good Night.

Recital

At intermission
She
Said, they're
Gone
You
Know.
Oh
Yes?
I asked
And
Raised
My
Eyes.
I used
To see spirits dance
Across the stage when I
Heard the violin. The sound
Has always embraced me, too,
Moved me back and forth with the
Bow. Wound a soft warm scarf about
My neck and shoulders, but
Never have I seen figures
prance on stage.

In the second half I held
Her hand and gently let our shoulders
Touch. The music rolled and swirled
Around but I was grieving for the
Dancers she had lost whom
I had never
Met.

Walking the Labyrinth at Rancho La Puerta

Daedalus, my co-conspirator,
Who built my labyrinth,
Ingenious, intricate, confusing
A walk too long to the center of my soul.

Where Midas, my king, there hid
The beast, half man, half bull
Who safely feeds on inner flesh
Protected in those awful depths.

And Theseus, the demigod
Half hero and half terrorist
By what right arrives and slays
My treasured Minotaur?

While Icarus confined
Escapes with knowing strength
But flies too high
And falls away.

Who am I, Pilgrim, who am I
As I walk this concrete floor?
You are all and you are none
But who to be today?

Shabbat in Cancer Land

T'was yahrzeit for my wife's mother and
The night before Purim,
The holiday of reversals,
Transformations.

Tale of deadly threat,
Evil and virtue,
Just desserts,
Perilous but fortunate.

We walked into the shul.
The shamus beckoned
Towards the table:
Challahs for healing.

Do you know these people?
Can you drop one off?
I looked at the tags;
My name was there.

The mishaberach came
And I called out,
Shachnah,
Shachnah ben David!

And I saw myself turning
And turning and turning,
For whom had the bread been baked?
It had been baked for me.

March

Retiring from the Canada FASD Research Network

We came to Canada to rest
We were offered work

We were asked to teach
But we were mostly taught

We arrived knowing a few folks a little
We are now embraced by friends

We arrived like most Americans knowing little about Canada
But assuming a great deal

We leave knowing a bit more about Canada
And have learned to listen first

My fundamental complaints about this land remain unaltered
Canada is just too big and I will never eat all the good food.

Still FASD remains epidemic
Innocent fetuses will be harmed tonight

Everyone in this room bears witness to the unfairness
Of this lifetime condition

I did what I could do to help
But there is so much more needs doing

I lift my glass to all of you
And bid you carry on

Mantra for Trainer Rachel

Lay down,
Let me stretch you
How is your shoulder?
Over there. Don't start yet.
Wait for me. Don't hurt yourself.
Wait for me. Relax your shoulders.
Slow
down.
Do it
Over,
Five
More .
Good
Job.
Slow
Down.
Engage
Your
Abs.
Nice
Job.
Head up. Wait for me. Over there.
Engage your abs. Elbows in.
Over here. Don't start yet.
I'm adding a quarter.
Okay, how many?
Six more.

Very good. Let me stretch you.
I'll see you Thursday.

Kahuwai Downpour

At last I can leave the beach
I do not need to snorkel or canoe
I do not need to seek out another
Bird whose name I do not know
Or look for shells or rocks
Or photograph a sleeping turtle

I don't need to apply the greasy film
That keeps the sun from killing me
I do not need to smile serenely
At the stranger in the abutting chair
Or make dreary conversation
Or even read my book

Even the plants are more active
Than I would like to be
Today the stones are soul mates
I will sit and let the waters
Splash upon my head and drip away
And come to terms with nothing

Make a Wish

I got a bow tie,
Blue umbrellas
On a sunny yellow field.
Ironic they tittered.

A bottle of single malt,
Old and dirty.
Just like you,
They guffawed.

Books about fishing in England
And mushing in the Yukon.
Thinner hopes for that now.
Not so, they cooed.

But a handmade book
For my scratches and
A really chocolate cake.
Then cards and calls from
Others I love.

And, well I am,
Grateful, you know,
For what I have.

Solace

The hawk was in the sky
As the curtained fog pulled away
So he could see the rocky gardens
And any movement of a beating a heart.

From the window I followed
His circling and circling of the hillsides.
Failing to find his breakfast,
He finally floated over the crest.

How casually he seemed to drift,
Calmly viewing the terrain,
Seeking the hare in the hedge
Like I the milk in a fridge.

Every flip of his wing seemed to say
Today will be like yesterday. The miracle of the
Hare will be repeated. There is nothing
Need be done but wait and watch.

Later, I did not notice when the door closed
Nor heard the foot steps in the hall.
The cut flowers in the vase evoked
No overwhelming sorrow for their death.

Today will be like yesterday.
What needs to be in place will find its place.
Oh, that the raptor of assurance could
Daily swallow the rodent of despair.

The Hex

Today is that day when
Spring won't stay outside
And bounds through the windows.

Yesterday's soft greens, yellows, pinks
Throb neon now, while
Lake and sky merge in the blue of creation.

Air sodden with wild perfume.
Can it do for bees what it does for me?
As finches sing the top to the jazz on the radio.

And I too must heed the murmur
That bids even the weeds to grow
Anew in the sidewalk cracks,

Try again, try again, try again.

The Wall

Scream
it is all right
Scream
no one can hear
as if you still care

Scream
let the pain, the stinking
pain
fill the air and suck it back
and let it cir cul ate

Let the pain
in your brain
fill your liver and your
lungs
see what your spleen can do
find real bile

Scream
let your muscles twitch
from phantom stabs
so real
that you will
Scream

Scream
cower in your bed
let the sheets be wet with
the sweat
oozing from the font of
your torment

It is what is
the final is is just the
Scream

Cheerios, Billy Collins and Being 70

Billy Collins wrote a poem about Cheerios,
When he learned that he was the same age.
Actually, he was just a little older than Cheerios.
He was 70 then,
The age I am today.
So Cheerios are older than I am.
I am happy that folks are still older than I am.
Some of you are part of that group, and
I am I happy that you are still here,
But older.
One starts to look around
For the ones who are missing
Or the ones too ill to make it
While one can still be here enjoying things.
But I must tell you the truth,
I never liked Cheerios.
Yet I have loved my life,
And my life with all of you,
And plan to read the back of the Cheerios' box
For many more years,
While eating my eggs.

April

The Miracle of You

i want to get up on the left side of the right bed
to wake first and watch you slumber
your hair loose on the pillow
your breathing untroubled soft

i want to turn again and hold you
to feel the movement of your
instinctive arm around my chest
to smell the sweetness of your skin

"Recital" Responsa

This is just to say
The magazine
Returned my poem
This morning.

They said it was not without
Merit, probably, like a boy scout.
Still they could not trust a walk
With it across the street.

So now I have received
My first rejection.
I shall treasure it,
So sweet and so cold.

Maui Day Break with Becca

The waves bathe the lava rocks
that drop into the sea
by the early morning light.
While turtles below await
Day tripping snorkelers.

"Did you know that I can say
three things in Maori?"
And puffy clouds erupt in the brilliant sky
as the kayaks paddle in
like a flock of noisy birds.

"No, I never knew."
Gently the breeze comes ashore
a riffle bounces the little boats
our coffees cool in our hands
even as the sun warms our heads.

"Do they eat papaya in New Zealand?"
I stand and move to the sandy edge,
the waters lapping at my feet,
waters that I'm sure have licked the
toes of small boys on a distance shore.

Absalom, oh, Absalom

Springing from behind the tree

Like a sudden puff of smoke
The shadow falling over the stone

Recoiling we like children,
Stunned and terrified.

You meeting the train head on.

Life should be more substantial,
Death harder to obtain.

You leave behind your days
for endless speculation.

Our anguish can't be buried
With your body.

Our doubts disrupt the peace
That you did endlessly seek.

May

Retired

I rise long after the sun
Still moving easy from the bed
No bell along the side
No one waiting

The day stretches open with
Rare an appointed hour
Yet all too soon the minutes fill
Busier now than ever

Things that I will do
Full of skillful pleasure
Please no one but myself
The jury's dismissed

I am resigned that
Life is harsh and rarely kind
And a smoky future beckons
I look square at entropy

Yet I search the news and talk
For bright ideas and new hopes
Saving money for grandbabes whose
Chances I will never know

They say I'm looking good
I know I'm still in some control
But if youth is wasted on the young
Experience is wasted on the old

Snit Fit

LISTEN TO ME
As I tell you about
MY feelings.

Up and down
Around and around.

You listen.

Doctor, tell me

When will I be dead?
When without voice?

Without breathe or beat?
Or thought or care?

When they put me in a bag
Or a box or an oven?

When no one can remember me?
Or when no one ever calls my name?

Or am I dead when the last
Of my genes is lost?

Why I hike

We climb the ridge
From valley floor
Out three miles
And up a half

Sunny and warm
Light breeze, no bugs
Good day, hard slog

To see the alpine farms
Transformed to miniature tableaus,
And birds

You walk in front
Swaying back and hips
And slender legs

All these years
And children grown
And still the most delightful view.

Tryst

Three AM when
Too True meets
Who Knows
Facing each other
Naked and afraid

Tumbling
Fumbling
Needy
Urgent

The world
So much more

Waking again
At dawn
Mask already
In place

To Sandy

What have you grown
As you grew?
You who made the bed.
You who were the bed.

Gardener and force of nature
You have always been so
Raising up and molding us
Shaking off the aphids

We could not help but feed
On your passion for the earth
Trees and flowers and chirping birds
Tidal waters and hanging vale,

Always with the keenest eye
For the plant that still
Needed pruning and the spot
That still lay fallow

We know like the hummingbirds
That you will warm the water
On the frozen morning
And always offer up a hand

We rise from you and go
We circle and return
We move forward because
We know from you what forward is

And now at 65
You are radiant with the life
That you have engendered in us all
We love you oh so much.

Outing

The boat moored on Sucia's shore
We search the fragile sandstone cliff
Rising straight from the Salish Sea.
Once it was the ocean floor now
Exposed and shorn by wind and rain.
Sediments blanketing mollusk shells
Nestled safe for an eon's time
Falling now, shattered chalky chards
Markers of thriving ancient life
Finally disappearing.

My wife espies a dinghy oar
Sadly dropped by a pleasure craft.
Clean and tossed upon the beach
She pulls it up and totes it home
And props it by the kitchen door.
To remember this, my birthday day
She says so smilingly

Out to Lunch

    Sitting in the café, Cactus,
    Physicians, retired,
    Cinco de Mayo,
    Drinking tequila at lunch.
    Why not?

    Settling in as old guys do,
    Wisely considering the weather,
    Touting a sporting team or two,
    Quoting a news commentator.

    Colleagues of a lifetime's work.
    Moving on to kids and trips,
    Books and shows, and a little gear
    While I am dreaming of a siesta.
    Why not?

    But then we speak of a friend who died
    And then another and then our own
    Dead folk – and then of us,
    and our firm plans for that.

    We have cared for many who
    Moved through to their ends,
    And bring to bear a tale or two
    That bolster what we think can be.
    Why not?

    We'd been there when it all went well
    And watched while things went so awry,
    Seen families stand tall and fall.
    Different paths to a common door.

    We sip the last and I know
    Each knows they really do not know
    How it will go when they face their time.
    But we will not discuss those fears.
    Why not?

June

Rebecca, Daughter of the Summer Solstice

The sun rises bright
On the longest day of light
A first grey hair falls

Wedding Dance

My brother called.
He asked me not to dance
The Kazatsky at his daughter's wedding
Because he thought I would.

Oh you know the Kazatsky,
That Russian dance,
You kneel with your bum
Just off the floor, your legs
Kicking forward one at a time
Or to the sides in rhythm to the music
The rest of you a bobber in the waves
Your arms folded across your chest
And you smile, that's important,
To smile and not to sweat.
I taught myself when I was young
I like to wait until there is a hora
And when the time is right
I leap into the middle of the circle.
I dance the Kazatsky!
I danced it at my wedding.
I danced it at my daughter's wedding
I danced it at so many weddings
And even some bar mitzvahs
No one ever asks one way or another
I just dance the Kazatsky.
My son has learned to do it too.
The only other soul I know who can.
Oh to dance the Kazatsky together!

But now there's been a coup.
My knees and balance and my neck
Have risen up and I cannot
Dance my dance again.
So when he called I wondered,
But then just said, all right.

Vincent Avenue North, Summer, 1951

"It's gonna be a real hot one today."
Gramps grumbled, while
Eating his perfect soft boiled eggs with toast,
Drinking his fresh perked coffee.

A breeze came through the window,
Reminding me to notice the cobalt sky,
The oak leaves dancing in the new day.
"Yep, really hot!" he scowled.

Summer Shower

    Strawberry shampoo
    Lemon shaving cream
    Spice deodorant
    Apple soap
    Mint toothpaste

    A fruit salad
    Exits the bathroom

Toast at a Family Wedding

Well, here is to Jeff and his bride Ginna,
He has surely picked a winna.
And here is to Ginna and her beau,
A finer man she does not know.

Everything is just so fine
And we're all having such a time.
The wedding tomorrow will be grand
And you'll go off then hand and hand

After you have said some vows and things
And traded pretty golden rings
And smashed a glass and kissed.
But there is something you might have missed.

Marriages lies like Persian rugs
On shelves in little dusty stores.
The strength of each is not seen
Until you roll them out upon the floor.

It isn't in the colors or the pattern
That you tell how they will wear.
It is in the woof and warp
And the meticulous care

That someone took with every stitch,
Every little knot and thread.
It's in the little things that make us itch
That marriages that last are bred.

Marriage is just kids and kinship
Bound with trust and tied by friendship.
It is a fragile weave without a loom
But there is no reason to feel gloom.

We know that you now know the task
And in each other you seem to bask
You share the needles and the thread
And relish the future that lies ahead.

So I'll sit down now and we will drink
Some wine and then we will think
About your looming, blessed life
And weaving through as man and wife.

The Carnival Ride

Around and around
And up and down
On the roller coaster
That has no stop.
Below I see the grey
Faced fathers who watch
With stolid gaze
Without gesture.
Falling toward the
Ground and whirling by
They look up and
Breathing out together
We cannot help you
We have nothing for you.
I hear no dog bark
But the caravan moves on.
I spin again around
Pulled to the top and
Dropped, again, afraid
I will crash
But, only swirling on.
A hatted crowd float
Beside and set a table
Lighting candles, pouring wine
Breaking bread
Intoning low. Words
I think I know.
Prayers to whom, for what?
Metaphors? No, NO!
Transformations
In and of themselves.
But the car does slow
And I leap and fall this time
Knowing soon the crash
And thinking all the time
Of how to roll on contact.

July

Canada Geese

A gaggle of geese,
Walking with their young,
Moving from pond to field,
Crossing the road.

When a truck from nowhere,
Speeding for no purpose,
Runs through their lines.
Striking four, driving on.

The living stand on the curbs
Looking into the street
Or looking away
Soundless, motionless.

Their bowels betray composure,
But they stand and stand.

I see all this as I walk with her.
She who does not say too much
Or smile anymore or even cry.
The new she who plods along.

And what of the mystery
That drove through her brain,
Striking her frontal lobes
And speeding off?

What can you do
When you don't know what to do?
How can you make sense of senseless?
Canada geese, my teachers

Bad Day for Butterflies

        Mountain ridge in mid July
        Too cold for butterflies
        The river trail muddy
        Water high and cloudy
        Hopeless dry fly fishing
        The birds seem hunkered down

        We stay by the fire
        Quietly poke at the logs
        Smokey fingers drifting
        No way to seek this place
        It just comes to us

Time for Healing

It is time to kill the elephant
She said as she took the gun
And handed it to me
To carry

It was a dewy morning
And the smell of early summer
And early hours lay
Teeming about

We walked through a sunny
Field along a gentle stream
To a bridge that I had
Never crossed

The town on the other side
Was made of cobble and mortar
Looking like burnished pewter
In the crystal light

Then the moist fresh scent of
Fruit and flower gave way
To the mid day heat and dust
Filled my nose

We walked through streets
Of shops and houses
But no one stopped to ask
Us what

The elephant was in the barn
On the edge of the town
In a cage in the barn without
Room to turn

The acrid smell of an animal
Penned by human chains in
The dark hot languid air
Stopped us

So I loaded the gun and I
Cocked the hammer and
Handed it to her to fire
The butt fell easily into place

An easy matter really to
Sight and fire
The elephant evaporated
Why so long

From Diablo Lake

                                    The
                                   trees
                                  ascend
                              the sheerest
                           ridge. Their taloned
                        roots grasp barest rocks.
                     It is not so steep they seem to
                   say. It is not so hard, not for you.

Life is a Beach

Can you wade in the shallows by the shore?
Stay upright when the waves crash
And the riptide pulls
Near the jagged rocks?

Falling will be disaster,
Standing will be standing.

Can you leave the water
And cross the dunes
And walk away and never
See this place again?

Walk, stay, fall, stand
Are these your choices?

Biking the Bay

    Flawless blue
        Above oaky leaves and maple
    Morning air crisp
        Caressing my brow
    Wheeling down this road
        Without effort
    I am nine again
        This moment is that moment
    I am frozen in time even as
        I fly, all breath and heart,
    From nowhere to nothing
        And fully there

Time Squared

At Hart's Pass I thought of Mary
Who'd lived in the valley below.
And flew off the ledge
Like the birds around me now.

Did she flit like these bluebirds,
Float like those swallows,
Dive like the hawk?

Could she smell the salt in the air?
Could she feel the heat from the ground?
How long was her fall?

If I only could remember Gravity's value,
If only I had measured the Height,
If only I had known.

August

Piggies

Four pigs at home.
When one left for the shops.
One had a nosh.
The others apparently were reading.

Then a fifth one cried
Wee, Wee, Wee,
And came running back.
Why was that?

Where had he been?
What scared him so?
Who assaulted or accosted?
How long had he been away?

Powerful thing running home.
Today I wouldn't know how.
Our building's sold, my
Goods sealed in cardboard.

There's been a price put on it all
But the value seems left somewhere --
In a dusty corner perhaps
Or under the sink?

Me and my piggies are starting the search
The packers left my bag with the ten essentials
But survival depends on knowing where to go.
The question remains open.

If I, like the little guy, cry
Wee, Wee, Wee
And just start running,
Will I get all the way home?

Poets on the High Divide

A band of prowling poets
Out with journals, stealing memories.
Inching across a talus slope
Noting bug, bud, fern and fly.
All had burst just melted snow
To gain a purchase on their brief season.

We are slower now than once,
Inserts in our shoes,
Poles to guide our steps.
Nursing knees and hips or squealing feet
Some have taken pills, some
Embrace the pain.

Happy to find the known,
Eager to name the rare
Peering through thick glasses
At this very new, old world.

The Decider

Which do you want?
I don't know.
Oh, what will it be?
I don't know.
Don't know or won't tell?
Don't know, don't know.
Will you ever be sure?
I don't know.
Can I pick it for you?
I don't know.
Won't you keep trying?
I don't know.
Could you be lying?
Oh no, oh no!

I am sick of this game
And sick of the sport
You must refrain
From another retort.
Please, oh please,
Do you understand
That we must find an answer?

I don't know.

August Question

In the summer,
Do you ever think
About a slog through snow?
Leaving tracks distinctly yours,
That fade to holes,
That fill with new snow
That melts too.

While boots dry,
Socks dry
Feet dry
Floors dry.

I think about that sometimes.

Red and Steamy

Unrelenting sun
Penetrates curtained windows
Room sweltering

Near the kitchen stove
Slowly she removes her clothes
Then strips his away

Their skins are rosy
Glistening with beads of sweat
Blood, water boiling

Floating in a bowl
Dark in the cool fridge
Lobsters sleep

They lead them then
From their peaceful slumberings
The caldron bubbling

They watch the creatures
Struggle and then quietly sink
In the roiling pot

Moving to table
All of them red and steamy
Soft bodies, hard shells

Breaking claws and tails
Violent with hammer and blade
Gently plucking meat

He stands before her
Placing hot flesh before flesh
He watches her chew

Dockside

The wee red-sided shiners
Rise from under the pier
Like evening stars over the hill,
One, ten, ten thousand.

I heave my feet among them.
They focus and respond.
Gently nibbling the corny skin
From my weary soles.

The old cutthroat trout
Observes the scene from below,
Considers his options,
Turns and swims away.

High Mountain Huckleberries

Head down on the mountain ridge,
Scanning small leaves on low plants,
Finding inky berries.
I look up when I hear the snort.

The large rock a few yards upslope
Now has a big, round face,
Two small eyes,
A yellow snout streaked blue.

We gaze at each other steadily.

Then snorting anew,
Throwing his head forward,
Rising to his feet,
His black body bounds up and off into the trees.

He leaves me the hillside and its spoils.
I leave them in turn for him.
Simple courtesies on the trail
As we are both content.

Syncope at the Country Concert

      A golden, gleaming afternoon
      Music bursting from the barn

      Thick honey scented air
      And cotton candy clouds

      Twelve swallows soaring
      In updrafts to down tempos

      And I hold your hand
      As you join the vapors

Cloudburst

The storm leapt the hill
Pounced upon us and
We ran without a path

Finding the old shed
Raindrops meeting the roof
Bursting like popcorn kernels

Trees swooned and
Swayed rubato
As birds spread their wings

Why did we not tarry
Letting the waters soak deep
How is it that we ran

Haiku in forest dusk

The bridge is solid
Made to survive the flood
But trembles with steps

In wind, the trees will
Sway together but they will fall
In time, one by one

Everything eating
Even now the mosquitoes
Make a meal of me

Ross Lake Sunrise

The sky smiled and the waters flickered as
I, lost among the bags and clothes scattered in the tent,
Peek beyond the zippered flap.

This place, as much as a man can love a thing
That is so much beyond the parts he names.
I sit and add myself.

Penultimate Poem

They say what fools
We poets be
Holding forth about a tree
Even stodgy docs
Can rhyme a verse
Slowly writing from
Bad to worse.

Yet gladden up
You reading folk
Most every topic
Is just a joke.

So see the world as
Big and bright
Or see the land as
Full of blight
Pick the style and
Choose the lore
And when you're finished
Just shut the drawer.

Cycle's End

Last evening's gloaming was ablaze
But fell quickly into inky night.
This morning's yellow warbler
Sat by my breakfast window
But wouldn't stay for lunch.
The still warm hands
Of the afternoon breeze
Now have cool fingers.

Fall is edging into the pool as
Summer is swimming away
Stroke by stroke and
I cannot go with her.
I'll take my brightest sweater
From the box tomorrow
I'll wear my trousers rolled
And walk along the shore.
Please come along.

Poems in alphabetical order

Absalom, oh, Absalom	65
Aging	33
August Question	99
Biking the Bay	92
Bad Day for Butterflies	87
Bampy Awaiting	14
Cabin Pressure	43
Canada Geese	86
The Carnival Ride	82
Cheerios, Billy Collins and Being 70	59
Cloudburst	104
Cuban Sunrise	32
Cycle's End	108
The Decider	98
Dockside	101
Doctor, Tell Me	70
Erev Rosh Hashanah and Jonathan	12
Family Fun	24
Friday night	36
From Diablo Lake	88
Haiku in the Forest	105
Happy 100th Birthday, Granny Pearl	29
The Hex	57
High Mountain Huckleberries	102
The Hunters of Playa Escondido	40
Jewish Eternity	15
Kahuwai Downpour	54
Life is a Beach	91
Make a Wish	55
Mantra for Trainer Rachel	53
Maui Day Break with Becca	64
May I be Excused?	41
The Miracle of You	62
New Years Morning	42
Nunavut Sojourn	22
Oh God, Oh No	25
Oh, Lord, it is I	34
Out to Lunch	75

Outing	74
Penultimate Poem	107
Piggies	96
Prenuptial toast for Katarine and Jonathan	28
Poets on the High Divide	97
Rebecca, daughter of the summer solstice	78
Recital	47
Recital Responsa	63
Red and Steamy	100
Retired	68
Retiring from the Canada FASD Research Network	52
Ross Lake Sunrise	106
Shabbat in Cancer Land	49
Snit Fit	69
Solace	56
A Stroll along the Nooksack	13
Summer Shower	81
Syncope at the Country Concert	103
Time for Healing	90
Time Squared	93
To an old Friend	44
To Sandy	73
Toast at a Family Wedding	84
Toast to the Marriage of Rebecca and Gregory	16
Transplant at 4811	37
Tryst	72
Upon Hearing of the Terminal Illness of our Mother	46
Vincent Avenue North, Summer, 1951	80
Walking the Labyrinth at Rancho La Puerta	48
The Wall	58
Wedding Dance	79
Why I Hike	71
Yahrzeit for David	18
Yom Kippur Reverie	23

Poems in chronological order

Jun 8, 2002	Summer Shower	81
Mar 12, 2003	Make a Wish	55
May 12, 2003	Why I Hike	71
Aug 27, 2003	Syncope at the Country Concert	103
Sep 15, 2003	A Stroll along the Nooksack	13
Mar 28, 2004	The Hex	57
Apr 21, 2004	Absalom, Oh, Absalom	65
Jul 11, 2004	Bad Day for Butterflies	87
Aug 31, 2004	Cycle's End	108
Sep 25, 2004	Yahrzeit for David	23
May 8, 2005	Tryst	72
Jun 4, 2005	A Toast at a Family Wedding	84
Aug 17, 2005	Cloudburst	104
Aug 19, 2005	Haiku in forest dusk	105
Mar 10, 2006	Kahuwai Downpour	54
Jul 2, 2006	Biking the Bay	92
Aug 20, 2006	High Mountain Huckleberries	102
Nov 25, 2006	Happy 100th Birthday, Granny Pearl	29
Nov 29, 2006	Aging	33
Dec 26, 2006	Transplant at 4811	37
Jan 2, 2007	Cabin Pressure	43
Jan 6, 2007	To an Old Friend	44
Mar 20, 2007	Solace	56
Aug 3, 2007	The Decider	98
Aug 4, 2007	August Question	99
Aug 23, 2007	Piggies	96
Mar 29, 2008	The Wall	58
Jun 15, 2008	The Carnival Ride	82
Jul 6, 2008	Canada Geese	86
Jul 18, 2008	Life is a Beach	91
Oct 1, 2008	Nunavut Sojourn	22
Oct 17, 2008	Oh God, Oh No	25
Feb 11, 2009	Recital	47
Apr 16, 2009	Recital Responsa	63
Jun 21, 2009	Rebecca, daughter of the summer solstice	78
Jan 20, 2010	The Hunters of Playa Escondido	40
Mar 8, 2010	Mantra for Trainer Rachel	53
Jul 1, 2010	Time for Healing	90

Date	Title	Page
Sep 11, 2010	Toast to the Marriage of Rebecca & Gregory	16
Jun 4, 2011	Wedding Dance	79
Sep 14, 2011	Bampy Awaiting	14
Nov 22, 2011	Oh, Lord, it is I	34
Dec 8, 2011	Friday night	36
Jan 1, 2012	New Years Morning	42
Apr 16, 2012	The Miracle of You	62
May 13, 2012	To Sandy	73
Aug 13, 2012	Red and Steamy	100
Sep 17, 2012	Erev Rosh Hashanah and Jonathan	12
Feb 22, 2013	Shabbat in Cancer Land	49
May 16, 2013	Snit Fit	69
Aug 15, 2013	Penultimate Poem	107
Aug 17, 2013	Dockside	101
Aug 18, 2013	Ross Lake Sunrise	106
Jan 5, 2014	May I be Excused?	41
Apr 23, 2014	Maui Day Break with Becca	64
Aug 1, 2014	Time Squared	93
Aug 2, 2014	Poets on the High Divide	97
Feb 13, 2015	Walking the Labyrinth at Rancho La Puerta	48
Mar 7, 2015	Retiring…	52
May 3, 2015	Doctor, Tell Me	70
May 13, 2015	Outing	74
Jun 26, 2015	Vincent Avenue North, Summer, 1951	80
Oct 14, 2015	Family Fun	24
Oct 31, 2015	Prenuptial toast for Katharine and Jonathan	28
May 1, 2016	Retired	68
Jul 17, 2016	From Diablo Lake	88
Sep 22, 2016	Jewish Eternity	15
Oct 5, 2016	Yom Kippur Reverie	23
Nov 17, 2016	Cuban Sunrise	32
Feb 17, 2017	Upon Hearing…	46
Mar 12, 2017	Cheerios, Billy Collins and Being 70	59
May 5, 2017	Out to Lunch	75

Glossary of Hebrew and Yiddish words used in some poems

Challah	The twisted egg bread typically eaten by Jews on the Sabbath
Erev	The eve and beginning of a holiday
Hora	An Eastern European circle folk dance
Lila	"Night" in Hebrew
L'Chiam	"To life" often said in a toast
Mishaberach	A prayer for healing recited in the synagogue while the Torah scrolls are opened.
Pushke	Family variant for a container for contributions to charity often given with a prayer.
Purim	The holiday celebrating the Book of Esther
Rosh Hashonah	The festival of the Jewish New Year
Schmoozing	Light social conversation
Shabbat	Sabbath
Shachnah ben David	The author's Hebrew name
Shamus	Literally "helper", may be used to refer to an usher at the synagogue
Shiva	A period of ritual mourning following a burial

Shofar	The ram's horn blown to announce the beginning of Rosh Hashonah
Shul	Synogogue
Simcha	A celebration
Tashlikh	The making of penitential prayers near water while tossing crumbs to fish or birds to signify the carrying away of sins
Yahrzeit	The anniversary of a death, typically commemorated at the synagogue by saying the Mourners' prayer and thinking about the life of the deceased
Yom Kippur	Jewish Day of Atonement

www.ingramcontent.com/pod-product-compliance
Lightning Source LLC
Chambersburg PA
CBHW072056290426
44110CB00014B/1708